Mind Your Manners
On Vacation

Núria Roca / Rosa M. Curto

BARRON'S

Hooray, vacation!

It's summer time, and Arnie and Sara are going camping with their parents. The sun is shining and it's a beautiful day. When Arnie looks for the things that he wants to take with him, he gets so excited that he bumps into doors and furniture. His sister laughs as she watches him. Arnie finally sees that he'd better calm down before he breaks something or hurts himself!

Fasten your seat belt

As soon as he gets into the car, Arnie fastens his seat belt. He notices something sticky in his hand. It's a gooey piece of candy. When Sara sees it, she remembers that it's the piece of candy that had dropped out of her mouth the other day! Now they understand why their parents limit what they can eat in the car.

Lunchtime

Mom and Dad have decided to stop for lunch. Sara and Arnie are tired of being in the car, even though they have been playing and singing. When she sits down to eat, Sara is so hungry that she does not remember to close her mouth to chew. She also doesn't sit down nicely or use a napkin to wipe her mouth. It's a good thing that Arnie reminds her about good table manners!

Good afternoon!

They have reached the lake. Right away, Sara starts asking other people questions—especially about bats, since she would love to see one at night. Arnie wants to ask questions, too, but he's a little shy and has trouble talking with people when he first meets them.

Lots and lots of dirt

This place is great! There is sand, rocks, water, grass, mud, and lots of kids to play with. Arnie and Sara get so dirty that they end up with sand in their hair, behind their ears, and even in their belly buttons! At night, Arnie's mom trims his fingernails so they won't be as long as a lion's or collect so much dirt! Sara tells her dad that her T-shirt is torn. It's time for the kids to climb into the bathtub and get clean again.

A day trip

Today the children will take a day trip to the mountains with their new friends. They wear hats and use sunblock to protect them from the sun. In their backpacks they carry some water, something to eat, and a small first-aid kit. The youngest boy wants to take a HUGE toy truck with him. The other kids tell him that he will get tired carrying it, and it wouldn't be fair if someone has to carry it for him.

Doing Chores

Even when they are on
vacation, Arnie and Sara still
have to help with chores. They
set and clean the table, empty
the trash, keep their belongings
in order, and make their beds.
They never feel like doing
chores, but Sara especially
doesn't like this today since
she has a cold. Arnie gives her
a tissue to blow her nose and
asks her not to "shower" him
every time she coughs or
sneezes!

Being different

This morning, a new family has arrived at the lake. There are two brothers: Marty, who is Arnie's age, and Pete, who is older. Pete can't jump or run very well or catch a ball like other kids can do. He's different. People sometimes laugh at Pete, but Marty explains why his brother is the way he is so they will not be mean to Pete. "But he whistles the best!" says Sara.

At the swimming pool

"No peeing in the pool!" warns Sara. "Of course not!" they all laugh. They have fun splashing one another, but they accidentally get a man all wet. They apologize, but the man is so angry that his face gets as red as a tomato. But he is right to be mad, isn't he?

The return trip

They are now back home. The children received a postcard from Rachel and Maria with a nice view of a beach. Maria said she was mad at her mom because she scolded her for running on the sand and bothering people. When she decided to look for shells instead, she got lost! Good thing the lifeguard helped her to find her parents. Wow! That must have been scary!

Silence!

Julia's family has invited Sara and Arnie to attend a puppet show. As soon as they get into the theater, Julia's little sister says she's thirsty. She wants her mom and talks all the time. She just can't sit still but tries hard not to bother everybody else. When the show is over, she is the one who claps the hardest. Bravo!

Animals

Arnie and Sara love all kinds of animals, but they are sorry to see them in cages at the zoo. There is a monkey that scratches its nose and another that eats a banana. Arnie wants to be a veterinarian when he grows up, and he knows that animals should not be bothered or fed by onlookers. Zoo animals are not tame pets.

Pillow fight

Sometimes parents like to go out by themselves, to see a movie or take a walk, so tonight, Sara and Arnie stay at their cousins'. They have pizza for supper, and when they go to bed, they have a pillow fight! What a mess. Now they can't find their pajamas, slippers, or the baby's teddy bear. They better put everything back in order before the grown-ups see what they have done!

Back to school

It's great going back to school, seeing friends and sharing the summer adventures. Norah and Betsy have traveled to Canada. Jim stayed at home because his grandma was sick, and his family helped to take care of her. Marty has learned to make kites, and Mark helped his parents paint their house. What do you think you will do when you are on vacation?

Activities

STAYING OVERNIGHT

Get your parent's permission to invite some friends to stay overnight at your house and make some pizzas for supper. Ask your mom to get pizza crust at the supermarket and help you prepare the ingredients to add on top: diced ham, olives, small chunks of sausage...whatever you like best. First you spread tomato sauce on the crust, then add your toppings. Finally, sprinkle grated cheese on top. After a grown-up cooks the pizzas for you in the oven, supper is ready. You'll love this pizza!

THE MIRROR

You need at least two players for this game.

You have to stand facing one another, because the game consists in imitating the movements made by the person in front of you, as if you were looking at a mirror. The second player (it may be your brother, dad, or mom) has to move an arm or leg, or make a face. The person who plays the mirror has to imitate the other person the best he can. He should not laugh, except if the other player does. After some time the players change their roles and the player who was "the reflection" becomes "the mirror."

NUTTY SHIPS

You don't need a windy day to sail your own ship! You can make a tiny sailboat, so small you can even put it in the bathtub. All you need is a walnut, a small rectangular piece of paper, and a toothpick.

Crack the walnut, eat the fruit, and keep half a shell. Using the toothpick, make a tiny hole in the upper and bottom side of the sail. Pass the toothpick through the holes to shape the sail and use a little plasticine or play dough to hold it in place inside the shell. If you make many ships like this, you will have a fleet of pirate vessels.

KNOCK DOWN THE TOWER!

You will love this game, you'll see! It's like bowling, only different. You need ten empty cans and pieces of paper in different colors to cover the outside of the cans. When you have them all covered with paper, pile them up to form a pyramid. Then gather several small balls. A tennis ball is ideal. The more kids who play, the more fun you'll have but you can play this game by yourself. If you play with someone else, be sure to take turns throwing the ball. The player who knocks down the most cans with just one throw (or one roll of the ball) is the winner.

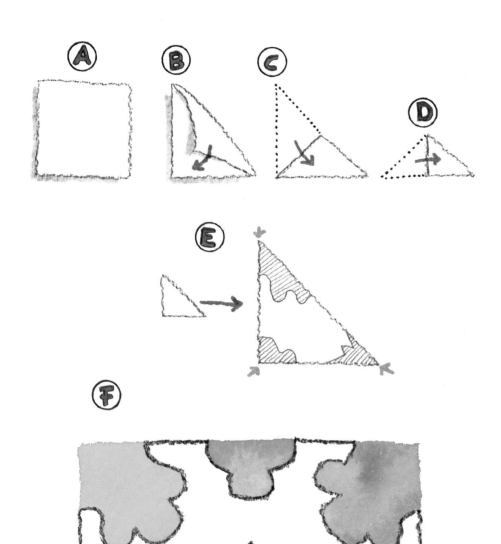

STAINED GLASS WINDOWS

Windowpanes that have different colors are very pretty, so here is a way to make your windows at home look beautiful.

Fold a square of black paper (or any other dark color) diagonally to make a triangle. Fold the triangle in half twice to make a smaller triangle. Cut off the three corners using different shapes. Unfold the paper and you will see your creation. Glue different colors of tissue paper or cellophane to the back of the holes. If you tape the square of dark paper to the windowpane, you will have a window that looks like stained glass.

Guidelines for parents

RESPONSIBILITIES

There is no need to make a long list of the things you would like your child to do. It will be easier for both of you to put him or her in charge of small tasks. For example, your child can be responsible for letting you know that he has dirt under his nails, which he can't get out, as in the section, *Lots and lots of dirt*. He can let you know if something breaks, gets dirty, or even if a button falls off his shirt. Don't carry on or scold him for accidents. Instead, ask him how it happened, and calmly let him know how you feel about the particular incident. It's important for your child to begin to feel responsible for his own belongings and personal hygiene within appropriate age expectations. He can gradually begin helping at home with small chores such as putting his laundry in the clothes hamper, putting shoes away, picking up toys, and when he is a little older, folding his clothes. To make chores easier, show him what goes where and make these places easily accessible to him. When children help, it often means more work for you! Remember that the effort is so worthwhile, since you are helping your child to become an independent individual.

HABITS

Daily habits are learned more easily and become automatic for children when there is some routine involved: eating at the same time every day, cleaning the table after meals, washing hands, brushing teeth, and so forth. However, if you don't like the regimentation of routine, you might choose other aids for your child, such as the use of drawings as reminders. Some suggestions include: the drawing of a toothbrush stuck to the mirror of the bathroom, a picture of a laundry basket on top of dirty clothes, or a photo of a single shoe that can't find its mate. It's often more effective to use a sense of humor than to argue and shout. When your child can read, you might use short reminding phrases such as a sign saying, "Got your sandwich?" posted

on the front door; this may eventually teach him to put his lunch in his backpack without reminders. Try not to be repetitive or overbearing since your child may begin to tune you out and resent the nagging.

WE ARE ALL DIFFERENT

In the section, *Being different*, we meet Pete, a child who is not able to do as many things as his younger brother. This is a good time to explain different kinds of disabilities and differences to your child. She may already have encountered people who cannot see well or those confined to wheelchairs. She may have also come across people who have emotional difficulties and demonstrate this by being inappropriately ill-tempered. Ask her to imagine how she might feel if she had to face these difficulties. It is so important for children to understand that we all have our strengths and weaknesses in physical, intellectual, and even emotional domains. We must find our own strengths and also see the talents of others: knowing how to listen, being understanding, learning a skill such as swimming or drawing, or even learning how to whistle really well!

SPACES OF FREEDOM

Young children should be allowed the space to be free from constant adult judgment and scrutiny. If safety is a concern with the very young, their activities can be monitored a bit surreptitiously! Now and then, they should be able to get dirty and not feel guilty if they get their shoes muddy or their clothes torn. While hygiene is fundamental, it is also necessary that children learn to take responsibility for themselves. Part of growing up involves taking moderate risks without constant adult supervision and scolding. Children who are overprotected and not allowed to make decisions can become either insecure or rebellious. It's also important that children understand that there's a time and place for everything. They can have fun and freedom but must not disturb others as they play. If children are exposed to different kinds of environments, they can learn to adapt their behavior accordingly and appropriately.

First English language edition for the United States and Canada published in 2005 by
Barron's Educational Series, Inc.

Original title of the book in Catalan: *Com ens hem de comportar durant les vacances*
© 2005 Gemser Publications S.L.
Author: Núria Roca
Illustrator: Rosa M. Curto

All inquiries should be addressed to:
Barron's Educational Series, Inc.
250 Wireless Boulevard
Hauppauge, New York 11788
www.barronseduc.com

International Standard Book No. 0-7641-3169-9

Library of Congress Catalog Card No. 2004111322

Printed in Spain
9 8 7 6 5 4 3 2 1